W9-AHN-728

SECRETS OF
POLLUTION AND CONSERVATION

ANDREW SOLWAY

Marshall Cavendish
Benchmark
New York

This edition first published in 2011 in the United States of America
by MARSHALL CAVENDISH BENCHMARK
An imprint of Marshall Cavendish Corporation

This publication represents the opinions and views of the author based on Andrew Solway's personal experience, knowledge, and research. The information in this book serves as a general guide only. The author and publisher have used their best efforts in preparing this book and disclaim liability rising directly and indirectly from the use and application of this book.

Planned and produced by Discovery Books Ltd., 2 College Street, Ludlow, Shropshire, SY8 1AN www.discoverybooks.net
Managing editor: Paul Humphrey
Editor: Clare Hibbert
Designer: sprout.uk.com Limited
Illustrators: Stefan Chabluk, sprout.uk.com Limited (page 5)
Picture researcher: Tom Humphrey

Photo acknowledgments: Alamy: p 29 (Wildlife GmbH); Corbis: cover penguin (Martin Harvey/Gallo Images), pp 5 (Charles R. Knight/National Geographic Society), 8 (HO/Reuters), 11 (Keren Su), 12 (Chinch Gryniewicz/Ecoscene), 14 (Ted Horowitz), 19 (Pichi Chuang/Reuters), 21 (Toni Albir/epa), 22 (Gideon Mendel); Getty Images: pp 4 (Andrew Holt), 15 (Hong Jin-Hwan/AFP), 20 (David McNew), 23 (Cristina Quicler/AFP), 24 (Cameron Davidson), 26 (Ron Erwin), 27 (Loungepark); iStockphoto: p 10 (Anka Kaczmarzyk); Aldon Scott McLeod: cover background; NASA: p 7; Science Photo Library: p 25 (Jerry Mason); Shutterstock Images: cover and pp 1 tiger (neelsky), 6 (Eric Gevaert), 9 (Alexander Kataytsev), 13 (SergioZ), 16 (Tish 1), 28 (Kim Worrell).

Other Marshall Cavendish Offices:
Marshall Cavendish International (Asia) Private Limited, 1 New Industrial Road, Singapore 536196 • Marshall Cavendish International (Thailand) Co Ltd. 253 Asoke, 12th Flr, Sukhumvit 21 Road, Klongtoey Nua, Wattana, Bangkok 10110, Thailand • Marshall Cavendish (Malaysia) Sdn Bhd, Times Subang, Lot 46, Subang Hi-Tech Industrial Park, Batu Tiga, 40000 Shah Alam, Selangor Darul Ehsan, Malaysia

Marshall Cavendish is a trademark of Times Publishing Limited

The website addresses (URLs) included in this book were valid at the time of going to press. However, because of the nature of the Internet, it is possible that some addresses may have changed, or the sites may have changed or closed down since publication. While the author, packager, and the publisher regret any inconvenience this may cause to the readers, no responsibility for any such changes can be accepted by the author, packager, or publisher.

Every attempt has been made to clear copyright. Should there be any inadvertent omission, please apply to the publisher for rectification.

Library of Congress Cataloging-in-Publication Data

Solway, Andrew.
  Secrets of pollution and conservation / Andrew Solway.
      p. cm. -- (Science secrets)
  Includes bibliographical references and index.
  ISBN 978-1-60870-140-7
  1. Pollution--Juvenile literature. 2. Conservation of natural
resources--Juvenile literature. I. Title.
  TD176.S6423 2011
  363.73--dc22
                          2010003943

Printed in China
1 3 6 5 4 2

Contents

How Have Humans Damaged
the Planet? 4

What Causes Air Pollution? 6

How Does Air Pollution
Affect Climate? 8

What Other Problems Does
Air Pollution Cause? 10

Does Land Pollution Affect
Lakes and Streams? 12

Are the Oceans Polluted? 14

What Do We Do With Fresh Water? 16

How Does Pollution Affect
Animals and Plants? 18

What Are We Doing About
Pollution? 20

What More Can We Do? 22

Can We Clean Up Polluted Areas? 24

Can We Protect Wild Habitats? 26

Does Pollution Just Affect
Individual Species? 28

Glossary 30

Further Information 31

Index 32

How Have Humans Damaged the Planet?

People have been living on Earth for about 200,000 years. For most of that time, the world population was less than a million people. However about 10,000 years ago, the population began to grow.

The Industrial Revolution

By the 1800s, the world population was more than one billion. People in Europe and North America began to make steel and steam engines.

Steam engines helped build bridges, railways, and ships, but they also caused **pollution**. These machines released smoke and harmful gases into the air.

▼ *Trees being cut down in a rain forest in Sumatra. Felled forests take decades to recover.*

▲ Mammoths disappeared about 10,000 years ago. The main cause was probably human hunting.

NOTHING NEW

Humans were causing damage to the environment well before the **Industrial Revolution**. Scientists think that hunting by humans as long as 45,000 years ago may have led to the **extinction** of mammoths, saber-toothed tigers, and other large animals.

The Twentieth Century

The pollution of the air continued into the twentieth century as cars choked the roads and airplanes filled the skies. Meantime, by 1999, the human population topped six billion.

What Next?

In this book, you will see how human activities are using up **resources** and damaging the earth. You will also discover what steps people are taking to restore the natural environment.

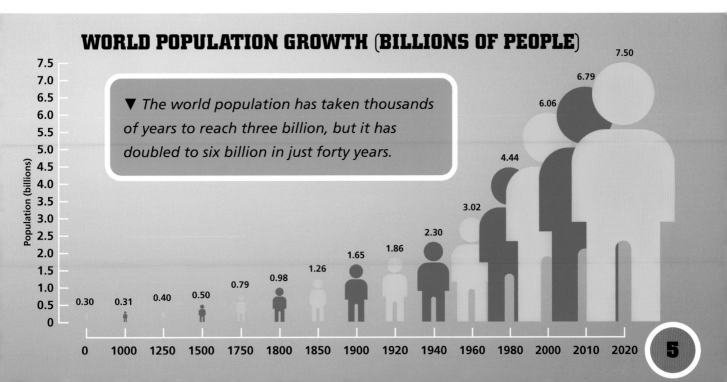

WORLD POPULATION GROWTH (BILLIONS OF PEOPLE)

▼ The world population has taken thousands of years to reach three billion, but it has doubled to six billion in just forty years.

Population (billions)

Year	Population
0	0.30
1000	0.31
1250	0.40
1500	0.50
1750	0.79
1800	0.98
1850	1.26
1900	1.65
1920	1.86
1940	2.30
1960	3.02
1980	4.44
2000	6.06
2010	6.79
2020	7.50

What Causes Air Pollution?

Burning **fuels** is one of the main ways that we get **energy**. We burn fuel to heat our homes, to drive cars, and to produce electricity in **power plants**.

Producing Smoke

However, burning fuel is the main source of air pollution around the world. It releases more smoke and gases into the air than any other human activity.

Other Sources of Air Pollution

Oil **refineries** and steelworks also produce harmful gases that escape into the air. Some factories, such as paint manufacturers, release deadly **vapors** into the **atmosphere**.

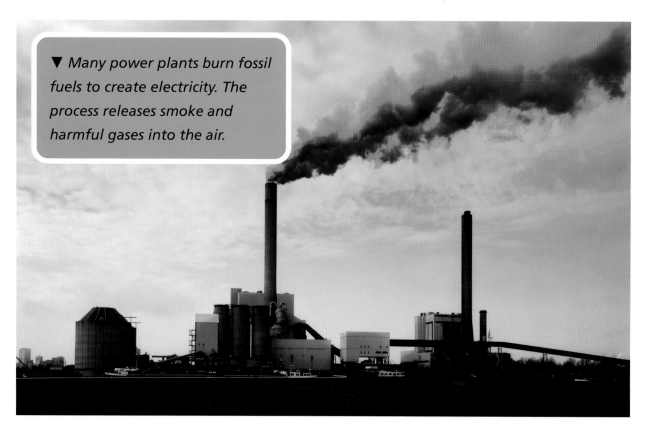

▼ Many power plants burn fossil fuels to create electricity. The process releases smoke and harmful gases into the air.

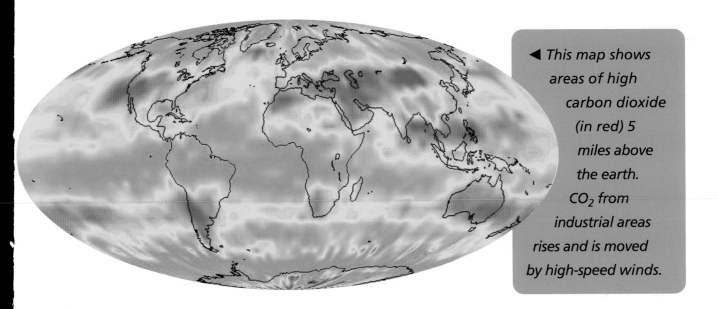

◀ *This map shows areas of high carbon dioxide (in red) 5 miles above the earth. CO_2 from industrial areas rises and is moved by high-speed winds.*

Gas and Smoke

Air pollution is mainly smoke and different gases. Smoke is made up of **particulates** (tiny particles of burnt material). It causes **smog** and makes it difficult for people to breathe. However, most air pollutants are gases:

INSIDE STORY

Air pollution is not just an outdoor problem. Tobacco smoke, gases from cooking, and vapors given off by paints and varnishes are some of the most common indoor air pollutants.

• **Carbon dioxide** (CO_2) is the biggest pollutant. It is given off whenever fuel is burned. So far, humans have released more than 350 billion tons of CO_2 into the atmosphere.

• When some fuels burn, they release **oxides**, such as nitrous oxide and sulphur dioxide. These oxides are also major pollutants.

• Persistent organic pollutants or **POPs** are produced by oil refineries and chemical plants. They are harmful even in small amounts, and they persist (stay) in the air.

• **Ozone** is an "active" form of oxygen. Gases from vehicle exhausts create ozone pollution.

How Does Air Pollution Affect Climate?

Climate change is the most worrying effect of air pollution. Scientists have shown that CO_2 and other polluting gases are slowly increasing temperatures around the world. This is known as global warming.

Carbon Dioxide

CO_2 is a **greenhouse gas**. It traps some of the Sun's heat close to the earth's surface, rather than letting it escape into space—just as the glass of a greenhouse traps heat.

Greenhouse gases are important for life on Earth. Without them, our planet would be too cold. However, CO_2 levels have increased by about 22 percent over the last one hundred and fifty years.

▼ *Some gases in the earth's atmosphere acts as a "blanket" to trap the Sun's*

Heat from Sun

Escaping heat

Heat trapped by atmosphere

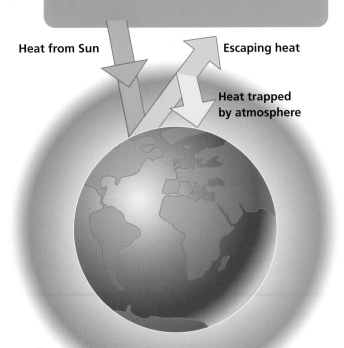

▼ *In 2009, the **Maldives** government met underwater to highlight the fact that the islands will be drowned if global warming continues.*

▲ *Herds of cattle produce large amounts of methane, which is a powerful greenhouse gas.*

Other Greenhouse Gases

Many other air pollutants are also greenhouse gases, for example **methane**, nitrogen, and sulphur oxides. Although these gases are released in much smaller amounts than CO_2, they have a more powerful warming effect.

SCIENCE SECRETS

METHANE ON THE FARM

Methane is released in large amounts by rotting trash in **landfill sites**, but most of it comes from farms.

Grazing animals, such as cattle and sheep, produce methane in their stomachs and release it in their burps and manure. A single cow can produce 17.5 cubic feet (500 liters) of methane per day. In the United States, more than 30 percent of all methane **emissions** are due to cattle and other **livestock**.

What Other Problems Does Air Pollution Cause?

Climate change is not the only bad effect of air pollution. Other pollutants cause damage to trees, freshwater fish, and other wildlife. Many are hazardous to human health.

Acid Rain

Some air pollutants, such as sulphur oxides, dissolve in raindrops and make rainwater slightly acidic.

In areas where a lot of acid rain falls, rivers and lakes may become so acidic that the eggs of fish and other animals will not hatch.

Damage to the Ozone Layer

The ozone layer is a region high in the atmosphere that is rich in the gas ozone. This blanket of gas absorbs much of the harmful **ultraviolet** (UV) radiation that reaches Earth from the Sun. UV rays can cause skin cancer and **cataracts** in humans.

Gases called **CFCs**, which were once used in aerosols and refrigerators, rise up into the ozone layer and destroy it. CFCs are now banned in many countries, but the ozone layer remains thin.

Since 1985, an ozone hole has appeared over the Antarctic in spring. People and wildlife in this area have little or no protection from UV rays.

◀ *Acid rain has damaged the spruce trees in this Polish forest. Most have lost their needles and some of the trees are dead.*

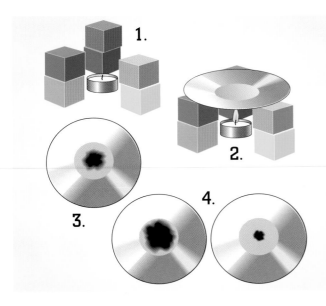

1.

2.

3.

4.

Smog

Ozone is helpful high above the earth, but at the surface it is a major cause of thick, choking smog. Smog is harmful to health, especially for people with **bronchitis** and **asthma**.

◄ Heavy smog over Shanghai, China.

SMOKY PARTICLES

This experiment will demonstrate how burning produces sooty particles.

You will need:
• small candles
• six wooden building blocks
• a metal plate • oven mitts

1. Arrange the blocks around one small candle so they can hold up the metal plate.

2. Ask an adult to light the candle, then carefully place the plate over the flame. After a minute, ask the adult to remove the plate, wearing oven mitts.

3. Wait for the plate to cool, then look at the surface. You should see a black smudge where the candle was. This is soot—tiny particles of carbon.

4. Try the same experiment with different small candles. Do some produce more soot than others?

Does Land Pollution Affect Lakes and Streams?

Many pollutants are soluble (dissolve) in water. When it rains, some of these materials wash away or drain through the soil into rivers and streams.

Mining Wastes

Miners dig up large amounts of rock from which they extract (take out) small amounts of metals or **minerals**. Often, the rocks are ground up and washed to free the valuable material. This process often releases poisonous **heavy metals**. The waste water flows into rivers or the sea, while the broken rock may be left in large piles.

Farming

Pollutants enter rivers from farmland, too. Many farmers try to boost crop growth by adding **phosphates** to the soil. If these get into rivers, they make plants grow too quickly and then die, clogging up the water.

▶ *Fertilizers containing phosphates have run off farmland into this waterway. Now it is overgrown with weeds and algae.*

Landfills

In many countries, domestic refuse is dumped in large holes known as landfill sites. Many modern landfill sites are carefully managed so that the wastes are contained and no pollutants escape. However, at older or less well-managed landfill sites, small amounts of heavy metals and other poisonous chemicals can be washed into the **ground water**.

▲ *A bulldozer buries food and other domestic waste at a landfill site. Much of this garbage could be recycled or* **composted***.*

EXPERIMENT

FROM LAND TO WATER

This experiment shows how ground water becomes polluted.

You will need:
• some uncooked rice • some salt • a small sieve • a bowl

1. Put some rice in the sieve and sprinkle a layer of salt on top. The rice represents the soil and the salt represents a pollutant.

2. Put the sieve under the tap with a bowl beneath it. Wash the rice with running water.

3. Taste the water. It will be slightly salty because the salt washed out of the rice and dissolved in the water.

Are the Oceans Polluted?

The oceans are so huge that it is hard to imagine them becoming polluted. That may be why they were used in the past as a dumping ground.

Dumping Garbage

All kinds of waste materials used to be dumped at sea. Coastal towns and cities got rid of their domestic refuse this way. Untreated **sewage** was also released into the sea. Developed countries now get rid of waste in other ways. They treat sewage before releasing it. However, many developing countries still use the sea as a dump.

GIANT GARBAGE PATCH

In the north Pacific Ocean, an ocean current carries plastic and other waste to an area known as the Great Pacific Garbage Patch. This floating garbage dump is over five times the size of the United Kingdom.

The trash harms wildlife. Sea turtles choke on plastic bags they have eaten, mistaking them for jellyfish, while lost fishing nets trap other marine life.

◄ Barges carry trash across New York Harbor. Until 1988, this waste was dumped at sea. Today, it is transported to landfill sites.

▲ *Volunteers work to clean up a massive oil spill in South Korea in 2007 after a tanker split apart.*

Mining wastes are often dumped into rivers or the sea. Some mining companies claim that this waste is safe, but there is evidence that it pollutes the waters, causing sickness and even death in local people.

Oil Spills

Some of the worst pollution at sea has involved oil tankers. A large tanker can spill millions of gallons of **crude oil** in a huge **oil slick**.

One of the worst tanker disasters happened in 1989, when the *Exxon Valdez* spilled 10.9 million gallons (41.3 million liters) of oil off the coast of Alaska. The oil slick covered 1,300 square miles (3,400 sq km).

What Do We Do With Fresh Water?

There are more than six billion people in the world today. Each person needs around sixty-five fluid ounces (two liters) of drinking water a day. However, many of us use far more water than this.

Water Usage

In addition to drinking water, we use water at home for cooking, cleaning, washing, and flushing the toilet. In developed countries, people use up to 130 gallons (500 liters) of water per day.

Even more water is used outside the home. Some industries require a lot of water, but agriculture is the biggest user.

In the United States, around 70 percent of the fresh water is used for **irrigation**. In many African countries, irrigation uses up more than 80 percent of the water.

▼ *Sprinklers water crops in a field. Irrigation systems use up huge amounts of water.*

Where Water Goes

Altogether, each person in a Western country uses 520–1,300 gallons (2,000–5,000 liters) of water a day.

Some of this water is cleaned in water treatment and sewage plants, and then released back into rivers or the ocean. However, water used for irrigation soaks into the ground and may not find its way back into rivers for many years.

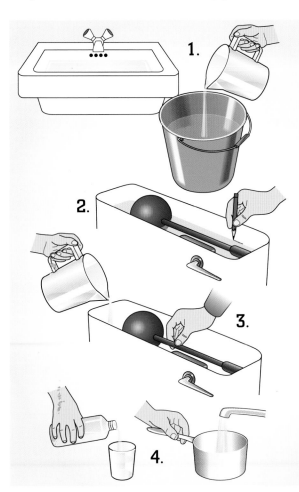

MEASURING WATER USE

In this experiment, you will measure how much water you use in one day. Ask an adult for permission before you start.

You will need:
• a 2-pint (1-liter) plastic measuring jug • a 18-pint (10-liter) bucket • a notebook and pencil

1. When you wash your face or shower, put the plug in the sink or bath. Use the jug to scoop out the water and measure it.

2. You'll need help from an adult to measure how much water you use every time you flush the toilet. First, lift the lid of the back of the toilet and mark the water level.

3. Now hold the float so it cannot drop, and then flush the toilet. Count how many jugs of water you must pour in to refill the tank to its original level.

4. Don't forget to keep a record of drinking and cooking water.

5. At the end of the day, add up how much water you used. Could you have used less water in any way?

How Does Pollution Affect Animals and Plants?

Wildlife and plants are often victims of pollution produced by humans. In some cases, the pollution gets inside their bodies.

DDT

DDT is a chemical discovered in the 1940s that was used as a **pesticide** (it killed insect pests). However, in the 1960s it became clear that DDT built up in the fat tissues of animals (for example, insect-eating birds) and caused them harm. All sorts of animals were affected, from fish and birds of prey to polar bears far away in the Arctic. People, too, have been affected.

DDT is now banned in many countries. However, even in places where it has not been used for forty years, people still have traces of DDT in their fat tissues.

▼ *The amount of DDT in plants and animals (shown in the yellow circles) increases higher up the food chain.*

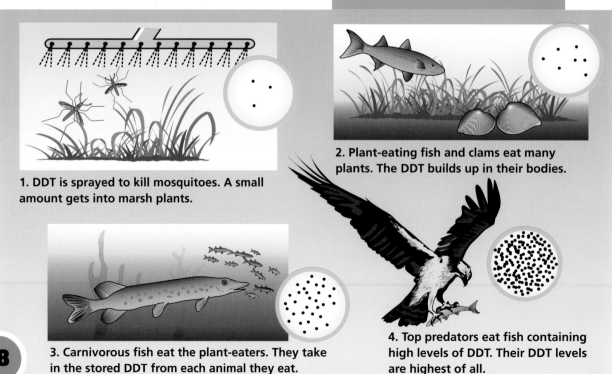

1. DDT is sprayed to kill mosquitoes. A small amount gets into marsh plants.

2. Plant-eating fish and clams eat many plants. The DDT builds up in their bodies.

3. Carnivorous fish eat the plant-eaters. They take in the stored DDT from each animal they eat.

4. Top predators eat fish containing high levels of DDT. Their DDT levels are highest of all.

🗝 HEAVY METALS

In several parts of the world, toxic heavy metals such as mercury, lead, and cadmium are affecting people's health. In some mining areas of eastern Europe, China, and Africa, the soil contains low levels of these heavy metals.

When food crops are grown on land that contains heavy metals, they take in the metals through their roots. Later, when people eat the food, the metals enter their bodies and can cause serious health problems, including damage to the brain.

POPs

DDT is one of a group of **organic chemicals** known as persistent organic pollutants, or POPs. Many POPs are used in manufacturing. All POPs build up in the fat tissues of animals.

In 2001, more than 150 countries signed the Stockholm Convention on POPs, promising to reduce levels of these pollutants. Since then, POP contamination has fallen, but there are still high levels in some animals.

▼ *Computers being recycled. Some parts can be reused, but they contain harmful substances. It can be dangerous work for the people doing the recycling.*

What Are We Doing About Pollution?

Pollution is a problem for the whole planet. One country can reduce its own pollution and waste, but it will still be hit by global effects such as climate change and water shortages.

Many people—individuals, scientists, politicians, and businesspeople—are working to reduce pollution.

Regulating Pollution

Governments and organizations such as the **United Nations** (UN) and the World Health Organization (WHO) have made laws and agreements to reduce pollution. Many countries have laws that limit the levels of pollutants in waste gases from factories and cars. These laws have led to cleaner air in cities.

Greener Businesses

New laws have forced factories to change the way they make products. For example, they cannot dump their wastes directly into rivers or the sea.

▼ *A plane sprays a field in California with a pesticide that is banned in most of Europe.*

▲ *Protestors dressed as aliens at the 2009 UN Climate Change Conference. They wanted governments to do more to stop climate change.*

Some businesses now make products that produce less pollution. For example, there are companies that sell toilet rolls, diapers, and other paper products made from unbleached, recycled paper. Not using chemicals such as bleach means less pollution.

Environmental Organizations

Many ordinary people concerned about pollution are involved in environmental organizations such as Friends of the Earth and Greenpeace. These groups draw attention to environmental problems and possible solutions.

SCIENCE SECRETS

SAVING THE OZONE LAYER

The Montreal Protocol, which came into effect in 1989, is one of the most successful agreements yet made to fight pollution. All the countries in the UN signed this promise to phase out the use of CFCs and other substances that damage the ozone layer. If countries stick to the agreement, the ozone hole should be healed by 2050.

What More Can We Do?

The problems of pollution get bigger as the world's population grows. We need to find ways of reducing pollution in the future.

Using Less Energy

The biggest cause of pollution is burning fuels for energy, so we need to try and use less energy. One way is to improve our buildings. Most buildings use large amounts of energy for heating and cooling, lighting, and to run household appliances.

By designing buildings with better **insulation**, we can drastically cut the energy we use in our daily lives.

▼ *These houses in Findhorn, Scotland, use far less energy than normal housing. Waste is reused or recycled, and most electricity comes from wind power.*

▲ *Mirrors direct sunlight at a solar power plant in Spain. The sunlight is focused on a huge boiler, which produces steam. This steam is then used to make electricity.*

Finding Alternatives

Some ways of producing energy cause more pollution than others. Most modern power plants burn fossil fuels such as coal, oil, or gas. In the future, we need to get more of our energy from sources that pollute less, such as sunlight and the wind.

Reducing Waste

Reusing or recycling waste materials is important, too. Food waste can be composted, and some organic wastes can even be used to make fuel. Metals, glass, paper, and plastics can all be recycled.

CHECK THE PACKAGES

Do we use too much packaging? Investigate next time someone in your house goes to the supermarket. As the groceries are put away, collect any discarded packaging and any old packaging that is being replaced. For example, if you get a new bottle of laundry detergent, the old bottle will become waste.

Look at your pile of discarded packaging. Was it all necessary? How much of it could be reused or recycled?

Could some of the packaging have been made differently to cut down on waste?

Can We Clean Up Polluted Areas?

In the last one hundred and fifty years, humans have changed Earth's ecosystems more than at any previous time in history.

We have cut forests for **timber**, plowed huge areas of land to grow food, dammed rivers to store water, and dug mines for metals and minerals. How difficult would it be to restore these ecosystems?

▼ *Conservationists have worked to restore the **wetlands** of Chesapeake Bay in the United States.*

Easy Recovery

Sometimes, removing the causes of pollution can be enough. Part of the **Great Barrier Reef** was almost destroyed by pollution. In 2006, the Australian government restricted fishing in the area and stopped the runoff of farm chemicals into the sea. These measures helped the **coral** recover rapidly.

▲ *The bacteria in these flasks can break down oil into carbon dioxide and water.*

The Power of Plants

Most polluted **habitats** need more help than this. In some cases, replanting native plant species is necessary. In parts of the Chesapeake Bay in the United States, for example, volunteers have replanted thousands of new plants in order to restore wetland areas.

Roots of Recovery

Plants can be used to **decontaminate** soil that contains mine wastes because they take in heavy metals through their roots. Plants such as ferns are grown, harvested, and then safely disposed of, leaving the soil free of contamination.

SCIENCE SECRETS

BEESWAX AND BACTERIA

A material called PRP, which was created by NASA scientists, has proved to be very good for cleaning up oil spills. PRP is a powder made of tiny, hollow balls of beeswax. The powder can absorb large amounts of oil.

The beeswax also attracts bacteria from the surrounding environment. These bacteria help break down the oil.

Can We Protect Wild Habitats?

Despite widespread pollution and the use of land for farming and building, many natural habitats around the world remain undamaged. We need to protect these areas, which are havens for wild animals and plants.

Northern Forests

Boreal forests once stretched in an almost unbroken band across northern Asia and North America. As well as being an important habitat, the forests are a **carbon sink**. The trees absorb CO_2 from the atmosphere.

Today, many areas of boreal forest have been cut for timber, or cleared for mining and oil exploration. However, Canada has banned logging, mining, and drilling for oil in large areas of its boreal forest.

▼ *Part of a protected area of boreal forest and wetlands in Newfoundland and Labrador, Canada.*

Replanting Trees

Since 1982, China has encouraged its people to plant trees, in an effort to reforest more than 5 percent of the country. Since 1982, over 42 billion trees have been planted—more than in any other country. The project also involves the creation of several nature reserves.

Protecting Wildlife

The Cardamom Mountains in Cambodia are home to many endangered rainforest species, including tigers, elephants, and Siamese crocodiles. Even though large areas are protected, damage is still being caused by illegal logging, hunting, and the building of dams for hydroelectric power. Environmental organizations are working with local people to protect the Cardamom area.

▶ *Asian elephants are among the endangered rain forest animals that live in the Cardamom Mountains, Cambodia.*

SCIENCE SECRETS

Not even national parks are safe from pollution. Las Tablas de Daimiel National Park in Spain was set up as a wetland reserve. However, most of Las Tablas has dried up, and the **peat** deposits in the area have burned.

Farmers in the area have drained the park's water supply. They have drilled thousands of wells to extract water for irrigation.

Does Pollution Just Affect Individual Species?

Pollution usually affects a whole habitat rather than individual species. However, focusing **conservation** efforts on one species can often help many others in the same habitat.

Sea Otters

Many conservationists have campaigned to save sea otters on the west coast of North America. In the past, sea otters were hunted almost to extinction. As a result, their **kelp forest** habitat was nearly destroyed by sea urchins that fed on the kelp. Sea otters eat sea urchins, but there were too few otters to control urchin numbers.

Today, sea otters are protected from hunting and the kelp forests have recovered. However, sea otters are still threatened by oil spills along the coast of Alaska.

▼ Sea otters were hunted for many years for their thick, silky fur. However, in recent years pollution from oil spills has threatened the species.

Protecting Vultures and Our Future

Indian slender-billed vultures are useful because they remove waste from garbage heaps. In recent years, however, thousands have died of kidney failure after eating cow carcasses contaminated with drugs. The vultures could die out completely, but conservationists are working hard to save them.

Rescuing endangered species is just one of the ways people are working to protect the earth. Human activities use too many resources, cause pollution, and destroy habitats. Working to reverse these changes is vital for our future.

▼ *Very few saiga antelope remain, because for years they were hunted for their horns.*

SCIENCE SECRETS

CONSERVATION MISTAKE

In 1993, there were more than a million saiga antelope on the **steppes** of central Asia. In the early 1990s, conservation groups encouraged hunting of the antelope for its horns. They were trying to protect the much rarer Asian rhinos, also hunted for their horns.

Unfortunately, the antelope were hunted mercilessly. Today, fewer than 50,000 saiga antelope remain, and their numbers are still falling.

Glossary

asthma A lung problem that makes sufferers wheezy and short of breath.

atmosphere The layer of gases around the earth.

boreal forest A type of conifer forest found in cold climates.

bronchitis A lung problem, sometimes caused by bacteria or other microbes.

carbon dioxide A gas that makes up a small part of the air, given off when a fuel is burned.

carbon sink Something that absorbs more carbon (usually in the form of CO_2) than it produces, for example some kinds of forest.

cataract An eye condition that causes increasingly blurred vision.

CFC Short for chlorofluorocarbon. One of a group of chemicals that were used in aerosols and refrigerators, but are now banned in many countries because they damage the ozone layer.

climate The general, long-term pattern of the weather in a region.

composted Turned into compost (a rich material made from rotted plants that improves the soil).

conservation The work of scientists and other concerned people to preserve disappearing habitats and living things.

coral A tiny living thing found in warm, shallow seas that resembles a plant, but is actually an animal. Many corals produce chalky coverings that build up into rocklike structures.

crude oil Oil in its natural state, before it has been refined (made pure).

decontaminate To remove pollutants.

domestic refuse The waste from homes, offices, and other small businesses.

ecosystem All the plants, animals, and other living things that live and interact in an area.

emission The escape of gas, smoke, or other pollutants from vehicle exhausts, factory chimneys, and other waste sources.

energy The ability to do work.

extinction When a species (type) of living thing dies out completely.

fuel Something that burns to produce lots of energy, such as heat.

Great Barrier Reef A 1,600-mile (2,600-km) coral reef off the northeast coast of Australia.

greenhouse gas A gas in the atmosphere that traps some of the Sun's heat.

ground water Water in the rocks below ground.

habitat A place where animals and plants live and grow.

heavy metal A metal such as mercury, lead, cadmium, and chromium.

Industrial Revolution A period in the late 1700s and early 1800s when countries in Europe and North America began to build factories and produce goods in large quantities.

insulation A way of reducing heat loss.

irrigation Providing farm crops with water.

kelp forest An area of ocean where very long, ribbonlike seaweed grows in large numbers.

landfill site A place where waste is buried.

livestock Cattle, sheep, and other farm animals.

Maldives A group of low-lying coral islands in the Indian Ocean.

methane A powerful greenhouse gas. Methane burns well and is sometimes used as a fuel.

mineral A simple material found in rocks which may be mined from the ground. Silica and quartz are common minerals.

oil refinery A chemical factory that makes fuels and other materials from crude oil.

oil slick An accidental spill of oil that floats on the surface of the sea or washes up on the coast.

organic chemical A chemical that is based on the element carbon.

oxide A substance made up of one or more elements combined with oxygen. (Elements are simple chemicals made of one kind of atom.)

ozone A form of oxygen that causes pollution in the lower atmosphere but also protects Earth from ultraviolet rays in the upper atmosphere.

particulate One of the small, light particles of burnt material in smoke and other emissions.

peat A heavy brown or black plant material found in the ground in bogs and swamps.

pesticide A chemical used by farmers to kill insects and other pests that destroy crops.

phosphate A substance that helps plants grow. Too much makes them grow fast and then die.

pollution The contamination or poisoning of the environment (land, air, and water).

POP A chemical (usually used in farming or industry) that does not degrade (break down).

power plant A factory that makes electricity.

resources Useful materials from the natural world, such as metals, oil, and salt. Food, water, and air can also be thought of as resources.

sewage Waste water from houses and factories.

smog A choking fog caused by air pollution.

solvent A liquid that many different materials can dissolve in.

steppes Large grassland areas that stretch across Russia and central Asia.

timber Wood used for building and carpentry.

ultraviolet light A form of light with a very short wavelength that is not visible to humans.

United Nations (UN) An international organization that works to improve how countries work together peacefully.

wetlands Marshy, boggy habitats.

Further Information

Books
The Atlas of Endangered Species by Richard MacKay (University of California Press, 2008)

Environment at Risk: The Effects of Pollution by Louise Spilsbury (Heinemann-Raintree, 2005)

Reducing Air Pollution by Jen Green (Gareth Stevens, 2005)

National Parks and Conservation Areas by Jen Green and Camilla Lloyd (Hodder Wayland, 2009)

Why Science Matters: Reducing Pollution by John Coad (Heinemann Library, 2009)

World at Risk: Resources by Andrew Solway (Franklin Watts, 2009)

World at Risk: Waste Disposal by Andrew Solway (Franklin Watts, 2009)

Websites
Go Wild
(http://gowild.wwf.org.uk/gowild/)
Information, games, and other interesting stuff about wildlife conservation from the WWF (World Wildlife Fund).

The IUCN (International Union for the Conservation of Nature)
(http://www.iucn.org)
The IUCN's red list of endangered animals, which is updated each year, as well as other useful information.

Pollution hotspots
(http://news.bbc.co.uk/1/hi/sci/tech/4083331.stm)
A news report on some of the worst pollution problems around the world.

Water Science
(http://ga.water.usgs.gov/edu/index.html)
What happens to freshwater in the United States? Find out all about it on this website from the U.S. Geological Survey.

Index

acid rain, 10
air pollution, 4, 5, 6–7, 8–9, 10–11, 20
asthma, 11
atmosphere, 6, 7, 8, 10, 26

bronchitis, 11

carbon dioxide, 7, 8, 9, 25, 26
carbon sinks, 26
cattle, 9, 29
CFCs, 10, 21
cities, 7, 14, 20
cleaning up pollution, 24–25
climate change, 8–9, 10, 20, 21
composting, 13, 23
conservation, 24, 28–29

dams, 24, 27
DDT, 18
decontamination, 25

ecosystems, 24
electricity, 6, 22, 23
endangered animals, 27, 28, 29
energy, 6, 22–23
environmental organizations, 21, 27

farming, 9, 12, 16, 19, 24, 26, 27
fertilizers, 12
Findhorn, Scotland, 22
food chains, 18
forests, 10, 24, 26
   rain forests, 4, 27
fossil fuels, 6, 7, 22, 23
fresh water, pollution of, 10, 12–13, 15, 20
Friends of the Earth, 21

global warming, 8–9
Great Barrier Reef, 24
Great Pacific Garbage Patch, 14
greenhouse gases, 8–9
Greenpeace, 21
ground water, 13

habitats, 25, 26–27, 28, 29
heavy metals, 12, 13, 19, 25
hunting, 5, 27, 28, 29

Industrial Revolution, 4, 5
industry, 4, 6, 16, 19, 20
insulation, 22
irrigation, 16, 17, 27

landfill sites, 9, 13, 14
laws, 18, 20

Maldives, 8
methane, 9
mining, 12, 15, 19, 24, 25, 26

nature reserves, 27
nitrogen, 9

oceans, pollution of, 12, 14–15, 20, 24, 28
oil refineries, 6, 7
oil spills, 15, 25, 28
oxides, 7, 9, 10
ozone, 7, 10, 11, 21

packaging, 23
particulates, 7
pesticides, 18
phosphates, 12
POPs, 7, 19
population, 4, 5, 22
power plants, 6, 23
PRP, 25

recycling, 13, 19, 21, 22, 23
reducing pollution, 20–21
refuse, 13, 14
resources, 5, 29

sewage, 14, 17
smog, 7, 11
smoke, 4, 6, 7
solar power, 23

traffic, 5, 6, 20

United Nations, 20, 21

water usage, 16–17, 20, 24, 27
wetlands, 24, 25, 26, 27
wildlife, 10, 14, 18–19, 26–27, 28–29
wind power, 22, 23
World Health Organization, 20